Levi Strauss
The Blue Jeans Man

ELIZABETH VAN STEENWYK

Also by Elizabeth Van Steenwyk

Dwight David Eisenhower
Three Dog Winter

Levi Strauss
The Blue Jeans Man

ELIZABETH VAN STEENWYK

WALKER AND COMPANY

NEW YORK

First published in the United States of America
in 1988 by the Walker Publishing Company, Inc.

Published simultaneously in Canada by Thomas Allen & Son
Canada, Limited, Markham, Ontario.

Library of Congress Cataloging-in-Publication Data

Van Steenwyk, Elizabeth.
    Levi Strauss / by Elizabeth Van Steenwyk.
       p.   cm.
    Includes index.
    Summary: Traces the life of the immigrant Jewish peddler who went on to
found Levi Strauss & Co., the world's first and largest manufacturer of denim
jeans.
    ISBN 0-8027-6795-8   ISBN 0-8027-6796-6 (lib. bdg.)
    1. Strauss, Levi, 1829–1902—Juvenile literature.   2. Levi Strauss
and Company—History—Juvenile literature.   3. Clothing trade—
United States—History—19th century—Juvenile literature.
4. Businessmen—United States—Biography—Juvenile literature.
[1. Strauss, Levi, 1829–1902.   2. Levi Strauss and Company.
3. Clothing trade.   4. Businessmen.   5. Jews—Biography.]
I. Title.
HD9940.U4S798   1988   338.7'687'0924—dc 19 [B] [92]   87-31809

Illus & Photo Credits
Pages 29, 38, 43, 51, 52, 59, 68, 71, 72, 73, 78, 81, 89, and 91, courtesy of
Levi Strauss & Co.
Page 15, courtesy of California State Library.
Pages 22, 25, 63, 86, courtesy of the Bancroft Library, University of
California.
Pages 33, 34, 65, courtesy of Department of Parks and Recreation, State of
California.
Page 46, courtesy of Western Jewish History Center, Judah Maagnees Memorial
Museum.

Book Design by Laura Ferguson

Printed in the United States of America

10 9 8 7 6 5 4 3 2

My special thanks to the following for their assistance, enthusiasm and friendship: Barbara Simon, Joyce Bustinduy and the other helpful staff of Levi Strauss & Co., and Tova Gazit, Ruth Raphael, and Mariam Aroner of the Western Jewish History Center.

Contents

Introduction

Gold! The word spelled fortune to the passengers leaning against the railing of a clipper ship as it sailed into San Francisco Bay on March 14, 1853. Since news of the discovery of gold had reached the rest of the world four years earlier, more than one hundred thousand people had traveled west in search of their future. Today, the clipper ship brought still more fortune seekers, all of them hoping to become rich.

Levi Strauss was among the people aboard the clipper ship that day. Since news of the gold rush had reached him some months before, he had been determined to join the thousands of adventurers eager to search for wealth in the hills of California.

Even back in 1847, the year Strauss had arrived in the United States from Germany, he may have expected to find gold in the streets of New York City. Talk in his native village of Buttenheim said that a man could easily find gold on his doorstep in the new land across the sea.

Strauss had journeyed not only across the Atlantic, but now around the continent of South America and up the coast of California as well. If he could find gold at all, he would surely find it here.

However, his fortune was not to be found in the hills. It would be found in his merchant's cases stored beneath him in the hold of the ship. In them he had packed fine silks and broadcloths, needles, threads, and scissors. He had also included rolls of heavy canvas for wagon covers and tents. His brothers, Jonas and Louis, 'who ran a store in New York City, had provided him with the merchandise and encouraged him to go west to search for wealth.

The ship sailed through the entrance to the bay newly named the Golden Gate by hopeful miners. It passed the many rotting hulls of ships abandoned by sailors who had joined their passengers on land, hoping to make it rich in the hills. More abandoned ships had drifted ashore to become restaurants or boardinghouses. Others simply had been pulled apart, their lumber used for building material, which was always in short supply.

Now small craft came from shore toward the clipper ship. As soon as the boats were close enough, men called out, asking for news of the East. Still others were eager to come aboard and look at merchandise that might be for sale. Levi was probably not used to such eagerness on the part of the buyers, but he sold nearly everything while he was still aboard ship and received pay in gold dust. All that Levi had left in his cases were bolts of canvas that he hoped to sell at a good profit to the prospectors needing shelter and transportation in the hills. No matter, he would send a letter back to Jonas and Louis, asking them to ship more fancy materials, needles, and other goods.

As the clipper passengers left the ship that day, they must have called goodbye and good luck to one another. It had been a long three-month voyage in cramped quarters on the trip around Cape Horn, with nothing much else to do but to talk. At least some of his fellow passengers knew Levi's name that day as he disembarked in San Francisco.

One day soon, however, everyone in the city would know Strauss's first name. And not many years later that name would become one of the best-known words to come out of the settling of the West. Even throughout the world, nearly everyone would know the name Levi.

1

A Modest Beginning

His name hadn't always been Levi. At his birth on February 26, 1829, in the small town of Buttenheim, Germany, his parents, Hirsch and Rebecca Strauss, named him Löb.

It is possible to trace the Strauss family back to the mid-eighteenth century, since not all Jewish records were destroyed in Germany during World War II. Birth recordings in the registers of the Jews of Buttenheim appear from time to time, beginning in 1741. The first Strauss, whose name was Jacob, appears in 1774, when his first son's birth was registered. A second son, Hirsch, was born six years later. The family address was listed as house 134 in Buttenheim.

Hirsch married Emanuela Schneider and had four children: Jakob, Jonas, Louis, and Mathilde. After the death of his first wife, Hirsch married Rebecca Haas and two more children, Fanny and Löb, were born.

Buttenheim was located in the beautiful area of Germany known as Bavaria. Thick forests covered much of the countryside, and mountains rose in the distance, luring those who had the time to quiet summer walks and boisterous winter games.

Buttenheim would have been a pleasant place in which to live if life hadn't been a daily contest for survival. The Strauss family struggled constantly against worsening economic conditions, growing political unrest in the country, and bigotry.

At that time in Germany, Jews were not allowed to own land, so farming and the raising of livestock were forbidden as occupations. Those Jewish heads of household who had some education entered positions open to them in the arts and sciences. Those who were without education simply took what was left over.

Hirsch Strauss was listed in the village registry as a dry-goods salesman, which in that day probably meant that he was a peddler. He was following an occupation that can be traced from ancient times, when Jewish peddlers from Antioch in Greece sold their wares to Caesar's legions in France and Britain. Among the most famous peddlers were Jewish women, who sold perfumes to the wealthy ladies of Rome. These perfume peddlers were among the few Jewish people who interacted directly with the powerful Roman women and influenced their lives.

The peddler enjoyed a similar position in the days of the feudal system of Europe. He moved from village to village while the townspeople seldom moved beyond their own boundaries. The peddler brought them news and gossip as he sold his wares and he had access to all, wealthy and poor, young and old.

ILLUSTRATION OF JEWISH PEDDLER FROM
HUTCHINGS MAGAZINE, HOLIDAY PICTORIAL,
1857—58.

Throughout the years, the peddler's position was enviable, yet difficult. Although he saw many people and visited many places, he also experienced extreme hardships including poor food, lack of proper shelter, and disease.

These hardships may have contributed to Hirsch Strauss's last illness, which was called consumption then. It was probably tuberculosis. When he died in 1845, his youngest son, Löb, was sixteen years old.

No one knows how the family survived during the two years following Hirsch's death. Two of the older brothers, Jonas and Louis, emigrated to the United States during this time.

Then, in June 1847, Rebecca Strauss petitioned the courts in Bamberg for passport and emigration documents to go to North America. The petition was granted in the same month. Shortly after, Rebecca, with the children Mathilde, Fanny, and Löb, journeyed north to the city of Bremen and boarded a ship for the new land. Soon now, Löb would have a new name as well.

The Strausses and others like them were among the first wave of immigrants coming from Europe in the mid-nineteenth century. Revolutionary outbreaks in the governments of European countries were chiefly responsible for the rising tide of people who left to better themselves in the New World.

Of the nearly two million people who would enter the United States by 1860, about five percent were Jews. Many who came were young and strong, since in Europe the number of Jewish marriages was severely restricted by law. Quickly the young Jews cast aside their old ways and joined in the American adventure, eager to begin businesses and families as well.

The Strausses' journey from Bremen to New York City lasted about four weeks. They traveled steerage class, which meant the lowest fare and the lowest position in the boat. At first they were seasick in their hot, cramped quarters. Then a day came when they got their sea legs and could stand on deck, watching and waiting for land. When they caught a faint scent of greenery mixed with the now familiar salt air, it was an impression never to be forgotten.

New York had a skyline even then, and it must have been exciting for those immigrants to know that their future lay somewhere in that city and beyond. When the boat docked, the passengers were processed at Ward's Island in the East River, where an emigrant hospital and refuge were located. There was no landing depot for immigrants until Castle Garden was established in 1855 in Battery Park. A guard spoke to them in German, giving instructions and ending with, "Welcome to America." They waited patiently as their papers were examined, and then the Strauss family was reunited with the two older brothers, Jonas and Louis.

2

A Prep School
for the Future

Jonas and Louis were not wearing polished boots and beaver coats, the clothing of the wealthy, the day they welcomed the rest of the family to America. They were not rich yet, but they expected to be and worked hard toward that goal. Levi was expected to join them in the family business. (His name was changed now; the reason is unknown.) Jonas and Louis were dry-goods salesmen—peddlers—as their father probably had been in Germany. The older brothers explained that peddling was an honorable occupation in America where Jews were given equal citizenship and could even vote.

18

Peddling in the New World was primarily the trade of recent immigrants, especially those from Germany and Scandinavian countries. The reason was simple; it was the quickest way for them to begin earning a living. Because the new arrivals could not yet speak English and because they felt they looked different, they had little chance of immediately being employed. Instead of peddling themselves to find a job in the marketplace, they peddled their merchandise. Through this trade, they were able to learn the language and the customs of the new country and to earn a living as well.

Levi Strauss wanted to belong to this new country as quickly as possible and soon began to learn English and the different ways of earning a living. Jonas and Louis were good teachers. They took their eighteen-year-old brother with them to the large supply house on Division Street where they selected their wares for resale to customers. Levi watched closely as they chose yarns and threads, needles, thimbles, combs, buttons, and scissors. They may also have bought larger items such as kettles, books, shoes, and bed linens. There were many household items from which they could choose.

Like all peddlers, each brother carried two packs hanging from his shoulders, one on his chest, another on his back. By Monday morning, the packs were crammed with as much as they could carry, and then all peddlers everywhere were off to the countryside for another week of selling.

In the United States, army commanders of frontier outposts took advantage of the peddlers and used them to negotiate with unfriendly Indians. They were among the few white men welcomed in Indian camps and settlements. Recognized as nonfighters, the peddlers were only bringing something to sell. Even more important, they were not settlers, they were just passing through. The Indians did not trust settlers, who were a threat to ownership of hunting grounds and grazing lands.

One tribe of Indians, the Cherokee, called peddlers "egg eaters." Because food offered to them was not prepared according to kosher dietary laws, Jewish peddlers had to refuse it. So wherever they went, they asked for eggs in trade, existing on a diet of eggs and vegetables until they returned home to a kosher kitchen.

Many of the Jewish peddlers arranged routes that brought them home in time to make proper preparations for the Sabbath. Sabbath was the Jewish day of worship and began on Friday night at sundown, lasting until the following day at sundown.

At first Levi traveled with his brothers to learn the way of peddling in the new world. They slept in barns and stables, always arriving back in New York in time for the Sabbath.

Soon though, Levi was working alone, making his own selections at the warehouse and fixing his own packs. It is said he traveled around the outskirts of New York, going as far as Pelham. Soon he paid back his brothers for all that they had loaned him to get started.

Jonas Strauss must have done particularly well, because, just one year later, in 1848, he was listed in Rode's *New York City Directory* as the owner of a store at 203 ½ Division Street. Louis was still listed as a peddler. Jonas's store prospered, and after three years the store moved to larger quarters at 165 Houston Street. During this time, Louis became a partner in the store.

Sometime during this period, Levi moved to Louisville, Kentucky, to live with a relative. It is not known who the relative was or why Levi moved there, except that it may have been considered prime territory for a strong, young man eager to make his mark on the world. He began to sell the goods from Jonas's store in New York and he probably spent about five years in the South.

Levi carried a pack weighing nearly one hundred pounds

as he tramped through the Kentucky hills. Each day he hoped to sell at least three dollars' worth of goods in the ten miles that he covered. Oftentimes the twenty-five-cent sales of needles and handkerchiefs didn't quite make his three-dollar goal, but he had an optimistic outlook. First he would make enough to buy a horse and wagon. Then he would make a fortune, as others in peddling had before him.

Thousands of peddlers used the trade to earn enough to start a permanent business, just as Levi's brothers had done. Others saved for more education that would provide a lasting profession. A New York doctor who once was a peddler said that peddling was the "prep school" of America.

In later years, Levi would hear of other successful merchants who once were peddlers. Benjamin Altman, Adam Gimbel, and Marshall Field became founders of large, well-known stores. And, in 1847, Meyer Guggenheim was a twenty-seven-year-old peddler, walking the back roads of the Pennsylvania coal country. Soon he launched a career in copper mining and became a millionaire many times over.

In general, any peddler's arrival was a special event in the lives of people living in remote areas of the country. Husbands came in from the fields, the children came in from play, the wives made up their lists of things to buy, and everyone listened while the peddler talked. He brought news of the area, perhaps from distant neighbors, and sometimes even brought a newspaper no more than a week or two old.

The one peddler who received the biggest welcome, who seldom encountered hostile farmers or situations, was the Jewish peddler in the South. The reasons were both religious and economic.

In the South, fundamentalist Protestantism was the pop-

ular religion of the day, with special attention given to the
books and teachings and heroes of the Old Testament. In
the small towns and villages where few people had ever
seen a Jew, the peddler was proof of the living witness of
the Bible. The peddler was Moses or Abraham in the flesh,
standing at the door.

Many people wanted to have the peddler as a guest for
the night, so that he could be questioned about his religion.
Fresh from their orthodox upbringing in the old country,
many peddlers, like Levi, were happy to comply, and the
Southern farmers looked forward to their coming with
respect and awe.

In his memoirs, Harry Richter, a former peddler, dis-
cussed this pleasant experience. He said, "In the South, the

orthodox Protestants granted us dignity; they were the first to make us feel that we really belonged." Levi's feelings must have been similar.

Later, after the Civil War, the Jewish peddler began to deal with Negroes who had recently been freed and were buying things for themselves for the first time in their lives. Men wanted hats and women wanted gold wedding bands. Often these items were paid for on credit. When their names went in the peddler's little credit book, it showed the world that they were paying their own way.

Before the Civil War, however, another event happened in the United States with historic impact as unsettling and nearly as catastrophic as the War. Gold was discovered in California in 1848, and the rush was on. Levi Strauss knew that he must be a part of that migration to the future.

3

"The buildings of this Sitty are generally rather poor."

LEANDER V. LOOMIS

Before the first prospectors docked in February of 1849, San Francisco, California, was a sleepy village of several hundred people who lived in clusters of adobe huts, tents, and shacks crowded together around the docks. One dusty path led out of town to the Mission Dolores and another to a military outpost called the Presidio. As more and more people arrived, the town began to spread out from these shore-front buildings and to move inland over sand dunes and chaparral-studded hills.

Late in the year, more than six hundred ships had been abandoned in the harbor. Two years later there would be

774, most with their cargo still aboard. An attempt was made to clear the harbor of these ships, but most of the hulls remained, to be surrounded and covered by wharves that extended into the bay. Sand eventually covered other ships' hulls.

As the city grew, the wharves became streets, and new extensions served the harbor. Citizens learned that it was easier to fill in the bay than to build on the hills. That would come later, when there was no place else for the city to grow.

By the time Levi arrived in 1853, the sleepy town had become a lively city of more than seventy thousand inhabitants. The city had already survived a series of disastrous

HIGH AND DRY.

STRANDED SHIPS WERE CONVERTED TO LAND USE IN SAN FRANCISCO IN EARLY GOLD RUSH DAYS. THE SHIP *NIANTIC* AS A HOTEL IS ON RIGHT.

fires and, after each one, rebuilt with fire-resistant materials. Iron and brick were used more and more, though bricks cost a dollar apiece, and lumber, when it was used, cost a dollar a foot. Assorted ships' parts were used as well.

Some years were to pass before the city would rid itself of streets that became rivers of mud when it rained. The few sidewalks were made of wooden planks thrown across muddy roads. Men could sink to their waists in them, and occasionally they and their mules drowned. At the corner of Clay and Kearney Streets, a warning sign appeared during one of the heavy autumn rains:

> This street is impassable,
> not even jackassable.

Levi stepped ashore that day in March to a city of "twenty-three wharves, thirteen ironworks, four sawmills, five theaters, nine billiard-table manufacturers, one hundred seventeen dry-goods establishments, twenty-eight breweries, and three hundred ninety-nine saloons."

It was a noisy, turbulent city and violent as well. By the end of summer, 1853, the coroner had recorded twelve hundred murders for the first half of the year. Many more people were thought to have died violently, because newcomers often disappeared as suddenly as they had come.

San Francisco was the gateway to the gold fields, and many people stayed only long enough to find passage to the mines. But others, like Levi Strauss, had no intention of going any farther to find their fortunes. Because there was such a demand for goods in the city, everyone became an instant businessman (and sometimes an instant millionaire) if he had anything to sell.

A man named Morris Shloss was just such a person. As soon as his baggage was unloaded onto the dock, a stranger approached to ask him what was in it. Shloss said that he had a wagon in the box, priced to sell at $125. The stranger said he would pay a hundred dollars for it, sight unseen. After paying for the wagon with gold dust, the stranger carefully opened the box, returning the wagon inside to Shloss. The stranger wanted only the box, to be used as his cobbler's shop in the daytime and his residence at night. Shloss had paid three dollars for the box, which was only seven feet in height.

The fortune seekers who journeyed west with Levi included farmers, merchants, clerks, doctors, ministers, gamblers, and lawbreakers. Like Levi, most Jewish immigrants who came to San Francisco were merchants. They quickly opened for business in flimsy shanties and tents crowded with goods shipped by relatives back East. Levi and his brother-in-law, David Stern, were the western end of a supply line that was quickly established with Jonas and Louis Strauss in New York.

San Francisco was a good place for recent Jewish immigrants to begin again. Here they had no struggle for acceptance by an established society, and their self-respect was not assaulted daily by unfair laws levied at them. The reason was simple. There was no established society and few laws showing prejudice toward anyone. Everyone came to San Francisco as equals in the early years, giving its new Jewish citizens a feeling of welcome and security they had not found elsewhere.

Although Jews and Gentiles coexisted commercially and sometimes socially, they would rarely intermarry. This was not due to religious prejudice, however, but simply because everyone learned to respect differences of faith and accept them as they were.

David Stern had come to San Francisco from St. Louis, Missouri, probably in 1851. He was married to Levi's sister, Fanny, and had also been a peddler in the Midwest. Sometime soon after Levi's arrival in San Francisco, the two men established their first shop, built on pilings near the Sacramento Street wharf. They may have reasoned that in a city of fire hazards there was no better place to be than near the water.

It was also the perfect place for beginning shopkeepers to watch for merchant ships arriving in San Francisco Bay. Levi knew that after their meager supplies were gone, they would have to buy more from the ships' auctions if they were to stay in business. They wanted to keep as customers the eager workers, gamblers, saloon keepers, and prospectors who began coming into the store.

The prices people were willing to pay for any merchandise at all were far higher than Levi had known back in New York. A package of needles he would have sold for one cent to a farmer's wife on his peddler's route now brought a quarter. A five-dollar blanket sold for forty here in this gold-crazed town.

The money Levi was paid for the goods he had brought with him was invested in new supplies at the auction houses until Jonas and Louis could replenish his stock. It took three weeks until his letter could reach them via the Pacific Steamship Mail Lines, which went across the Isthmus of Panama by mule or horseback and downriver in boats poled by natives. Once at the Gulf of Mexico mail, cargo, and passengers were loaded onto steamships for the final part of the trip to New York. The return trip around the Horn continued to be as long as four months for goods from New York arriving to replenish Levi's empty shelves. And there was no guarantee of that. Ships continued to be lost in the high seas of the Strait of Magellan.

In the meantime, the auction houses were lively places of business where goods shipped by eastern speculators to San Francisco wholesalers were stockpiled. Just about anything could be purchased: food, clothing, tools, building lots, even mining claims. There was plenty to be had one

LEVI STRAUSS AT ABOUT THE AGE OF 40.

day, practically nothing the next. Everything was a gamble. Profit, when there was any, could be anywhere from one hundred to five hundred percent.

Levi and David soon hired a lookout to watch for the arrival of merchant ships. Boys of eleven or twelve were employed by the local businessmen to spend their days on the hills above the city, watching through spyglasses for ships to appear far out in the bay. When the lookouts saw a ship approach, they ran to tell their employers.

Then Levi and David knew they had a day's head start before the ships docked in the bay and unloaded their cargoes into the auction houses. During this time, the merchants marked down prices on everything in the store and sold as much as they could at reduced prices. Businessmen in their circumstances couldn't afford to keep goods at normal prices during a time when supplies were readily and cheaply available at all stores. Only the wealthiest, with money in reserve, could keep prices constant.

4

> ## "A mine is a hole in the ground owned by a liar."
>
> **MARK TWAIN**

The story of how Levi made the first pair of sturdy work pants from the canvas that was ordinarily used for tents and wagon covers has been told with several variations. The following version is probably the most interesting.

When Levi arrived, he couldn't help noticing that the miners he saw on the street and later in his small shop were not only dirty, but ragged and shoddy. The clothes they had brought with them from their former lives were not sturdy enough for their new occupations.

The idea of making pants from tent canvas may have come from Levi or from a miner who was tired of losing his small stake of gold dust through a hole in his pocket. But it was bound to happen. The market was recognized by Levi, an intuitive marketing man, and a new product was born.

The miner apparently was happy with his new pants made from canvas and went about town advertising, free of charge, Levi's tough pants. Meanwhile, Levi had taken the rest of the canvas to the tailor who had made the first pair of pants and instructed him to make more. He was fairly certain that a brisk business would follow.

It did. Business continued to improve and by 1856 Levi and David moved to a larger store, up the street from the old one. Above the door at 117 Sacramento Street they hung a freshly painted sign that read "Levi Strauss & Co." They might have named the company "Strauss Brothers" since Levi and his two brothers, Jonas and Louis, and brother-in-law David were full partners. But someone else, not related to them, was already using that name on a Dupont Street dry-goods store. Since Levi had the best head for business in the family, his name went on the sign above their entrance. And so it remained.

Levi Strauss & Co. continued to grow as Levi added a new wrinkle to his clothing and merchandising business. He decided to become a wholesaler as well as a retailer, and his customers would be the other store owners out in the diggings. Once again he hit the road as a peddler.

News of gold's discovery in 1848 had traveled quickly. One year later, a living chain of mining camps and towns spread like mushrooms from north to south on what is now California's famous Highway 49. The names of those settlements were as colorful as the people who inhabited them. Boneyard Meadow, Shirttail Canyon, Rough and Ready, Groundhog's Glory, Bedbug, and Henpeck City were a few of the more memorable. Other camps such as New Chicago and Sonora were named for their citizens' origins.

The settlements followed the dislocated spine–like curves

of the Sierra Nevada where gold was hammered out of rocks, dug from mines, and washed from creek beds by the human wave of gold seekers who flooded the area.

Some miners came with provisions such as tents and food, pickaxes and spades, washbowls and rockers, hammers and drills, and enough gunpowder to blow up the Rock of Gibraltar. Many came without anything at all. They arrived armed with hope and little else.

Sonora was settled by miners from that state in Mexico. Because of the richness of the gold veins nearby, this camp quickly became one of the largest settlements on the Sierra slopes. The town's seven hills were covered by tents and hovels, and its main street wandered through a valley for one mile.

But there was only a narrow trail to the outside and the nearest supply base was in Stockton, seventy miles away. A decent meal couldn't be bought in Sonora, even with a gold nugget as large as a tortilla. Food was in short supply

AN EARLY DRAWING OF COLUMBIA, TWO MILES
FROM SONORA.

AN EARLY PHOTOGRAPH OF A CHINESE PROSPECTOR, 1852.

34

everywhere for a simple reason. When the rush began, fields and crops were abandoned by farmers and ranchers, who were as eager to dig for gold as anyone else. When the crops in the fields died, no one bothered to replant. Food soon became scarce until supplies were brought in by ship, often from as far away as the Hawaiian Islands. Prices, as a result, were prohibitive.

As the first winter began, half the town's citizens were ill with scurvy. To their credit, the miners quickly organized a municipal government so a hospital could be built in their wilderness town. Soon it was crowded with patients eating raw potatoes priced at a dollar fifty a pound and drinking lime juice at five dollars a bottle, the usual treatment for scurvy in those days. Doctors in the diggings charged from sixteen to fifty dollars per visit. In the city they charged only eight dollars.

News of the scurvy scare raced through the diggings and out to the rest of the world, but word of the unbelievable gold strikes spread even faster. The mob of miners increased, especially in Sonora. During the spring and summer, it was said that the route from Stockton to Sonora was easily traceable at night by the glow of campfires stretching for seventy miles.

The first Jewish people came into the diggings as old-fashioned pack peddlers, carrying shovels, knives, boots, and smaller items to the miners. However, the loads they carried were enough to flatten a mule. Often they dragged their packs uphill and rolled them down on the other side.

Quickly they found the Old World custom of going out to the countryside with a pack on one's back too impractical for the distance and terrain of the gold country. There were other discomforts and dangers as well. Several Jewish peddlers traveling alone had been scalped by Indians. Others became the victims of desperadoes or disease.

Soon many of the peddlers set up flimsy, jerry-built

stores in the mining towns. Three former peddlers, the Levinsky brothers and Charles Steckler, were attracted to an area where their route passed a deep, clear spring. When they and other entrepreneurs set up makeshift stores along a road nearby, the town of Jackson was quickly established.

Others did as Levi did; they bought a wagon and mule and sold their dry goods to the store owners who had settled down in one place. Levi's samples were packed in large trunks on the back of his wagon as he traveled up the Sacramento River by sidewheeler to the new capital of the state. From there he followed the wagon paths to out-of-the-way places such as Michigan Bluff, where Leland Stanford was a retail merchant.

When he first heard of California gold, Stanford was an attorney in Wisconsin. After his law library burned in a fire, he decided to head west for the golden hills rather than buy new law books. From his modest grocery in Michigan Bluff he moved on to bigger businesses and, finally, politics. Later, Stanford became a governor of California and a partner in the Central Pacific railroad, driving the last gold spike to complete the intercontinental line on May 10, 1869. Stanford University in Palo Alto was built with his fortune and named in honor of his son.

Levi may have met others who began their careers in small stores along the gold-rush highway. In 1849, Domingo Ghiardelli, an immigrant from Italy, began to build his fortune by selling groceries from his store in Hornitos to the miners of the area. After he left Hornitos, Ghiardelli started the chocolate company that still bears his name.

When John M. Studebaker came out from Pennsylvania to the gold-rush town of Placerville, he began to make wheelbarrows for the miners. After he had saved four thousand dollars, a considerable sum then, he returned to the Midwest and opened a wagon-building business in

South Bend, Indiana. Soon he was a millionaire. The wagon business was later converted to an automobile factory and, for years, Studebaker cars populated the highways.

Still other now-famous business names had their origins in the gold rush. Philip D. Armour began as a butcher in the Sierra hills. Later, he established a meat-packing business that exists today. John B. Stetson, who became a leading hat manufacturer, served his apprenticeship in the diggings at Shaws Flat. Mark Hopkins immediately organized the New England Trading and Mining Company in the East when news of the gold strike reached him. Then he set sail for California to protect his modest investment of two thousand dollars in the company. By the time he had finished building the Central Pacific railroad with his partners in 1869, his two thousand dollars was worth twenty million.

No one knows how many of these men were acquainted with Levi, yet they all could have been friends because of their common goal. In this new rough-and-tumble world, they were dedicated to earning their fortunes and securing their futures.

It was strictly a man's world out in the diggings for the first few years of the gold rush. After a while, however, even the strongest men were starved for the sight of a woman and for any symbol that might remind them of home. Young men, those in their teens particularly, were known to tramp for thirty miles just to see a mother and her children living in a remote mining camp.

For Saturday-night entertainment, miners joined in the dances as they had at home, but here they were forced to choose from their own stag lines for partners. When singers and actors arrived from San Francisco to put on a show, they were met at the edge of town and carried through the streets as if they were national heroes. Later, during a performance at the theaters, the entertainers were showered with gold dust.

Even itinerant preachers were greeted warmly, but more for their entertainment value than for their religious message. Religion was not on the minds of most miners. As one stated, "When I left home in Missouri, I hung my religious cloak on my gatepost until I should return."

For Levi Strauss, however, it was business as usual up and down the gold-rush highway. He continued to notice the ragtag miners and the clothes they wore and reminded himself to order more sturdy material for overalls when he got back to the store in San Francisco. If someone asked for a particular piece of merchandise that he did not at present carry, he made a mental note to order it before his next visit. He treated his customers as he would his friends.

EARLY MINERS WEARING LEVI'S JEANS.

Strauss's business kept growing, and soon he hired other salesmen to travel to the diggings. He may have reflected that they had an easier time than he when starting out. They carried no heavy packs nor gave away precious spools of thread in thanks for meager orders.

Their accommodations were certainly more pleasant too. True, they stayed in no fancy hotels, but at least they slept indoors. They didn't spend the night by the side of the road, hidden in brush near a creek as Strauss once had back East, fearful of strangers who might rob him of a few cents' profit while he washed his socks in the stream.

Soon, Levi wouldn't travel the salesman's route at all. He would stay in San Francisco and leave the selling to others. Now, however, he looked forward to the end of each trip and a return to the home he shared with his sister, Fanny Stern, her husband, David, and their growing brood of children. It seemed to be a good life for him, surrounded as he was by his business and family. For a poor immigrant boy from Germany who had no trade and little education, he was doing very well.

5

Rude Justice
and Polite Society

Levi's growing business had already survived San Francisco's first major economic crisis before it moved into its new quarters up the street. For a city so in love with gold and growth, it didn't take an earthquake to rock its none-too-secure financial foundations. On February 22, 1855, one San Francisco bank shut down because it simply could not give its customers the money that they had deposited. Several more banks closed the following day. The news spread like swamp fever, and people all over town panicked, withdrawing their savings from other banks as well. The domino effect toppled more and more banks as the panic spread. Banks were not prepared to pay out deposits to so many people at one time. Now businesses began to shut their doors, too, as their money was lost in banks that ran out of funds.

By the end of the day, many of the city's banking firms had collapsed, and half of the city's forty-two banks never recovered from that "Black Friday." Many businesses never recovered either.

But Levi had no problem. He knew the value of hard work and understood how to seek out a need in the marketplace and fill it. Soon now, his business would outgrow even the larger store at 117 Sacramento Street.

There were occasional times of stress, however. In 1856, San Francisco's second Vigilance Committee had been newly organized, and rude justice ruled the streets.

Rapid expansion from the early days of California provided fertile ground for the growth of a vigilance philosophy. Angry citizens had petitioned Congress earlier to set up a territorial government. This would replace the military law inherited when the Cahuenga Capitulation finally ended Mexican rule over California on July 13, 1847. But Congress was locked in debate over slavery, and little was done. Two years later, when the territory was overrun by gold miners, there was still neither government nor law enough to keep the new rough-and-tumble citizens in line.

Mining settlements adopted their own form of frontier law and ethics, but so many executions occurred in a town named Placerville that it was called Hangtown until late 1850. The more established towns turned over power to sheriffs and *alcaldes*, or magistrates. When they were honest, the law was honest. When they weren't, neither was the law. In this climate the first Vigilance Committee was formed in San Francisco in 1851.

Jews joined this committee because it represented the only organization that seemed to be on the side of law and order, and because they distrusted their city government, which was frequently corrupt. Never mind that the law and order the vigilantes represented was mob rule—it was the only rule in town. The frontier journalists of that day, however, preferred to call it "popular justice."

Jesse Seligman joined the Vigilance Committee in 1851 because, he wrote, "it was unsafe for anyone to walk the streets without being well armed, for there was no telling at what moment one would be attacked by the thieves, thugs, and desperate characters that had overrun the city."

MINERS AT LAGRANGE MINE IN LEVI'S JEANS.

The first committee disbanded after one hundred days of rule, and for a little while San Francisco endured fewer crimes. Several years later, however, local politics had sunk lower than the pilings in the bay, and citizens agitated for a new committee of vigilance to be organized. In less than a week, a committee had formed a tight military organization with headquarters at 41 Sacramento Street, less than a block from Levi's business.

They piled up such a barricade of sandbags that the building became known as Fort Gunnybags. Behind that five-foot wall, the members of the committee tried and condemned two murderers and hanged them from the second story of the Truitt Building. No one interfered with this quick justice, but to immigrants like Levi who could remember the treatment of Jews in Europe during pogroms, the hanging must have seemed an ominous sign.

In August, after nearly three months of activity that came close to pitting city and state against one another, the second Vigilance Committee disbanded. Many law-abiding citizens must have been as relieved as Levi when a true law-and-order government was finally restored.

As the violence that had been a part of the brawling city's existence began to lessen, its citizens yearned for a normalcy they had left behind in their other lives. Jewish newcomers in particular were lonely in the early years. They had no homes or synagogues, few had brought their families, and they did not even have a gathering place.

August Helbing resolved to change all that with his idea for a self-help society that could also be a social club for lonely Jews in San Francisco.

As Helbing recorded in his memoirs:

We Jews had no way of spending our evenings. Gambling resorts and theaters, the only refuge then existing in the city, had no attraction for us. We passed the time back of our stores and oftentimes were disgusted and sick from the

loneliness of our surroundings. Besides . . . every steamer
brought a number of our co-religionists . . . some came
penniless, having invested their all in a passage to the coast.

And so, in 1850, the Eureka Benevolent Society was
born. Dues were minimal, the membership grew, and it
became David Stern's favorite philanthropy as he and Levi
Strauss contributed generously through the years.

Now there was a social organization, but still no house of
worship. Lewis Abraham Franklin's large tent store had
been used for the first Rosh Hashanah, celebrated in San
Francisco one year earlier, in 1849.

Seventeen Jews, sixteen men and one woman, gathered
in Franklin's dry-goods tent-store on a September evening
to observe the High Holy Day. Since there was no Torah
scroll in the city, they used a Pentateuch to conduct the
services. A Pentateuch is the first five books of the Old
Testament, usually found in book form rather than as a
scroll. Someone read from it in Hebrew, they offered
prayers, and the brief service ended. Some years later, the
tent-store would become an historical landmark.

A similar service was held the following year, but it was
not until Passover, 1851, that an attempt was made to create
a permanent congregation and build a synagogue. However,
an ancient rivalry between German-born Jews and Eastern
European Jews began to bubble like an underground
spring. German Jews considered themselves superior to
those born in Poland and elsewhere.

The problem finally rose to the surface when a committee was formed to hire a *shochet*, or ritual butcher, for the
kosher slaughtering of meat. Each side proposed a candi-
date, and neither would give in to the other. The problem
was hopelessly stalemated and finally halved the citizens
into two permanent groups.

Two congregations were then formed along former national lines, Emanu-El for the German Jews and Sherith

TEMPLE EMANU-EL, SAN FRANCISCO.
THE CORNERSTONE WAS LAID IN 1864.

Israel for those born east of Berlin. Sherith Israel's first building on Stockton Street was not as large nor as grand as Emanu-El's first one on Broadway, and its cemetery was not considered nearly as fashionable either. For a few years, however, the two congregations shared a rabbi, and so they came to terms, although the rivalry continued as each congregation insisted it was the oldest in San Francisco.

Disagreement over following the Orthodox ritual divided the Emanu-El group from the beginning. In 1855, the Reform faction won out, and the congregation became one of the first to endorse the liberal resolutions of the Cleveland Reform Conference of Rabbis. In 1863, the group that preferred the stricter Orthodox procedures separated to start its own congregation.

Levi was a member of the Reform faction of Emanu-El congregation and, though he never held office, he was considered a noteworthy example of the virtues taught by religion. With Louis Shloss, Levi contributed the gold medal given annually to the best Sabbath School student, on the condition that his name not be used as the donor of the medal.

The 1850s were good years for Levi, his family, and his business, despite financial setbacks in the nation and occasional social ostracisms in the city. The national panic of 1857 did little to upset the growing dry-goods business on Sacramento Street.

The Sunday-closing law, established by the State of California in 1858, fixing the Sabbath on the first day of the week rather than the seventh, made little difference to Levi's business. His establishment was open six days a week, from six A.M. until six P.M. As a member of the Reform Temple of Emanu-El, he simply adjusted his early Orthodox training to life in the new world.

The slander voiced by Dr. John T. McLean must have been harder to take. McLean was a medical doctor, now a special agent of the Treasury Department, charged with collecting customs duties in San Francisco. When he was questioned about the low rate of collections, McLean replied, "A large portion of our underevaluations are found to be made by that class of people—German and French Jews. I think the Israelites a little more prone to that sort of business than persons who are not of that religious persuasion."

The Jewish citizens of San Francisco were rightfully angry and responded with a powerful broadside. "He [McLean] is a professional man, a doctor of medicine, and by accepting an inferior and not-too-honorable government office, he has virtually proclaimed his inability to earn an honorable support by the practice of his profession but does not hesitate to malign those who do, and who contribute to the public weal instead of slandering others."

The fact that this response was made at all shows the new strength and security of the city's Jewish citizens. In their former lives in the Old World, they would not have dared voice their objections on threat of harassment and/or imprisonment.

Levi Strauss was secure enough in his life now not to be troubled at all.

6

"The capital of the awakened Pacific"

Levi, with his brothers Jonas and Louis, his brother-in-law David Stern and another brother-in-law William Sahlein, now concentrated their efforts in one wholesale jobbing and manufacturing company. Central headquarters were in the new building at 14–16 Battery Street in San Francisco, with Eastern sales and manufacturing offices at Jonas and Louis's store in New York City. Levi spent twenty-five thousand dollars to finish the interior of the new building, designed with gaslight chandeliers, a cast-iron front, and a patented freight elevator. Completed in 1866, the building contained four floors of domestic and foreign dry goods, clothing, and household furnishings. More employees were added as the business continued to grow.

Levi now established a routine that he followed for much of the rest of his life. Each morning at nine o'clock he left the home he shared with the Sterns at 317 Powell Street on Union Square and started off to work. He walked the eight blocks to Battery Street, his black hat fixed securely on his head, enjoying the brisk outing. On the way he often stopped and spoke to friends and business acquaintances, for Levi was well-known in the city now.

He arrived at the office by ten o'clock each morning and immediately asked for the sales figures from the previous day. Then he spent the rest of the morning speaking to customers in the store on buying trips, or with stockclerks and bookkeepers in the offices and shipping rooms. He felt there was no better way of finding out what was going on in his business than keeping in touch with those people closest to the customers. Levi also discovered it was an opportunity to find the most eager clerks who were willing to work hard and earn promotion in the company.

Upon first meeting him, Levi's employees were usually nervous. After all, his name was on the building sign outside. But his five-foot-six stature was not imposing. His dark hair and neatly trimmed beard were no different from those of many other businessmen of the day. Only his heavy-lidded eyes may have seemed remote. However, when the employees found he preferred being called Levi to Mr. Strauss, they relaxed and were able to talk to him more easily.

After he had eaten lunch, Levi often attended meetings of other organizations in which he was interested. He was beginning to buy real estate and invest in the gas company, and he had become involved in businessmen's committees.

In the afternoon he returned to the Battery Street building and settled down at his desk in the large office he shared

LEVI STRAUSS & CO., 14—16 BATTERY STREET, SAN
FRANCISCO, SHORTLY AFTER THE BUILDING WAS
CONSTRUCTED, PROBABLY AROUND 1870.

51

with his bookkeeper, Philip Fisher. Mr. Fisher was also a close friend, and together they carefully went over the financial books and answered the mail.

Levi left his office around five o'clock, leaving Philip Fisher to close it an hour later. Levi then met a friend, usually Barney Schweitzer, and they would spend an hour or two discussing the day's events before going home. If Levi wasn't meeting friends for dinner that evening at a good restaurant or hotel dining room, he remained at home with Fanny's family. They were his family, too, and a large one at that. Eleven lived there most of the time—Fanny and David Stern; their seven children; Jonas's oldest son, Nathan, there from New York to learn the business; Levi; and sometimes Louis, visiting from the East.

LUMBERJACKS APPEAR IN LEVI'S JEANS.

As Levi walked around the city, his short figure was not outstanding among the many businessmen also walking briskly home or to social engagements at that hour. Most men of that day who had gained prosperity through their growing businesses wore black broadcloth suits with split-tail coats and top hats made of Japanese silk. Levi was no different.

Now as Levi moved through San Francisco's gaslighted streets at dusk, he saw that it bore no resemblance to the frontier outpost to which he had come only thirteen years before. The first five years of the gold rush alone had produced more than $285 million. These riches were turning San Francisco into a commercial and industrial capital. Richard Henry Dana, the author of *Two Years Before the Mast*, called it "the sole emporium of a new world." He also said, "the Jews are a wealthy and powerful class here."

The men who had made fortunes in the gold rush, either directly or indirectly, were building mansions in the area already known as Nob Hill and acquiring fine furniture and good manners to complete the picture of genteel dignity.

Culture was in fashion, too, as art galleries, libraries, social and literary clubs, and newspapers became well established. The demand for news was great because of the city's isolation from the rest of the country. Many citizens were qualified and ready to write and publish the news. Soon, early San Francisco claimed more published newspapers than London, as 132 newspapers and six literary journals appeared in the 1850s. Most of them lasted no more than a year, however, due to a lack of advertisers and paper, and often lacking employees. Sometimes entire staffs quit to go to the mines, and occasionally an editor was thrown in jail. The editor of the *Bon Ton Critic* was convicted of grand larceny and sent to San Quentin, an event noted by his newspaper just before it folded completely.

The quality of that early journalism was not the best

until those with real talent began to appear in the 1860s. By this time Levi was well established in his business and may have had some leisure time to read the words of young American writers who were beginning their careers there. Mark Twain, Bret Harte, Joaquin Miller, and Ambrose Bierce would move on from this time in western history to create illustrious places for themselves in American literature.

Other cultural advantages of city life, such as theater and restaurants, were available to Levi. Pantomimes, ballets, circuses, and dramatic plays were often performed by troupes of actors who stopped in San Francisco on their way to Australia. Particular favorites at that time were troupes of child actors, including one group of thirty who performed as the Marsh Juvenile Comedians.

One of the special favorites of miners in the diggings was another child, Lotta Crabtree. She began giving performances at the age of eight and went on to become a favorite in San Francisco and the East, both well-known and wealthy as a comedienne. When she died, she left four million dollars to charities.

In the late 1850s and early 1860s, new types of entertainment were being advertised. Live elephants, horses, crocodiles, and Chinese jugglers attracted the curious. So did magic tricks, tightrope dancing, and an India-rubber man.

After the performance, one of the city's many restaurants was always open to cater to every appetite. No opportunity was ever lost by a San Franciscan to create good food. Dr. Charles Parke, a local physician, found himself traveling through a mountain blizzard once when he decided to add oil of peppermint to the milk he was carrying on the back of his wagon. When he arrived at his destination, the jostling of the wagon on mountain roads had churned the milk into peppermint ice cream.

Sourdough bread also got its start when miners baked

their own bread over the glowing embers of their campfire, always sure to leave enough raw dough set aside to start a new batch. In cold weather the miners often took the pot of sourdough starter to bed with them to preserve its rising capabilities.

But it was the business and commercial life of San Francisco in which Levi was especially interested. Most of the businesses begun in the early years of the gold rush were based on products of necessity, in an economy based largely on dust. Gold dust. But the most capable business-men outlasted that stage.

Soon the bankers, the assayers, the jewelers, and insur-ance brokers moved to Montgomery Street along with bookstores and newspapers. Leather, equipment, machin-ery, textiles, and lumber became local products rather than imports from the East.

In 1854, the city converted to gas lighting and installed three miles of gas lines and eighty-four street lamps. Along the city's gaslighted streets, Chinese vegetable peddlers moved among the men and women hurrying to their homes or entertainment. Just beyond Montgomery Street, thirty thousand Chinese, or Celestials, called twelve blocks of Dupont Street home. Hundreds were crammed together in two oversized cellars running under Bartlett Alley and Washington Street. A ladder was used to gain entrance. The Celestials slept in rotation in these rat-infested places and worked for as little as a dollar a day. Chinatown's back alleys were as dangerous as any found in the world, and the area was roped off to prevent any unknowing Caucasians from wandering into it and oblivion.

The Civil War had ended just before Levi built his new building on Battery Street. Although the rest of the coun-try had been locked into this war during the years from 1861 to 1865, San Francisco seemed almost unaffected. The expense of moving troops to the battlefield in the East discouraged the Union Army from using California men, and the draft was never enforced, probably for the same reason. Volunteers from California did participate, however, among them Isaac Magnin, whose wife founded, in 1876, a well-known department store bearing his name. Definite feelings were expressed about the war, and, in Southern California, sympathy was shown for the Confederacy.

Citizens of San Francisco and the mines tended to be pro-Union, however, and rallies for the North were held in the downtown park that came to be known as Union Square. Rabbi Dr. Elkan Cohn of Temple Emanu-El supported the Union from the pulpit and fell down "as if in a faint" when the news of Lincoln's death reached him during services. The synagogue was then draped in mourning. Philo Jacoby, editor of *The Hebrew*, one of San Francisco's several Jewish newspapers, was a fervent supporter of Lincoln.

In California, and in San Francisco particularly, Jews had found a real promised land—a good climate, economic opportunity, and social and political equality. They tended to be patriotic and loyal to the federal government. A few years later, the patriotic stand of American Reform Judaism would be stated in a speech by Max Lilienthal, a gifted writer and public speaker, when he said, "All our affections belong to this country which we love and revere as our home and the home of our children." The pioneer Jewish community of San Francisco echoed those sentiments.

Levi Strauss, in the late 1860s, was a part of the Jewish community of San Francisco, a part of the business community, and a part of the cultural life as well. But these elements were not enough for him. His business, in his own words, was his "sole happiness."

7

"The secret of them Pents..."

JACOB DAVIS

Levi Strauss must have been happier than usual on the day he received an interesting letter from a tailor in Reno, Nevada, who was also a customer of his company. It was about business, so it seems reasonable to assume that a letter outlining a way to enlarge Levi's business would also enlarge his happiness.

The letter was written by Jacob Davis, or rather, written for him, with Jacob dictating the words. A Jewish immigrant from Riga, a city that had belonged to any number of European nations, Jacob spoke German as his first language and was none too certain about writing in his second, English.

So a druggist friend in Reno was entrusted to write a letter to Levi. On July 2, 1872, Jacob said that he was remitting a check for the balance he owed Levi Strauss & Co. Then he went on:

> I also send you by Express 2 pcs. Overall as you will see one Blue and one made of the 10 oz Duck which I have bought in greate many Peces of you, and have made it up in to Pents, such as the sample.

> The secret of them Pents is the Rivits that I put in those Pockets and I found the demand so large that I cannot make them up fast enough. I charge for the Duck $3.00 and the Blue $2.50 a pear. My nabors are getting yealouse of these success and unless I secure it by Patent Papers it will soon become a general thing. Everybody will make them up and thare will be no money in it.

> Tharefore Gentlemen, I wish to make you a Proposition that you should take out the Latters Patent in my name as I am the inventor of it, the expense of it will be about $68, all complit and for these $68 I will give you half the right to sell all such clothing Revited according to the Patent, for all the Pacific States and Teroterious, the balince of the United States and half of the Pacific Coast I resarve for myself. The investment for you is but a trifle compaired with the improvement in all Coarse Clothing. I use it in all Blankit Clothing such as Coats, Vests and Pents, and you will find it a very salable article at a much advents rate . . .

> These looks like a trifle hardly worth speakeing off but nevertheless I knew you can make a very large amount of money on it. If you make up Pents the way I do you can sell Duck Pents such as the Sample at $30 per doz. and they will readly retail for $3 a pair.

To the experienced eyes of Levi and his partners, this read like an interesting and worthwhile business proposition. Levi Strauss & Co. ordinarily sold workingmen's pants for around ten dollars per dozen wholesale. Jacob

Davis charged $30.00 just by adding a few rivets, which could only have cost him a penny or two.

The partners acted quickly. One week later, Levi's attorneys sent Jacob patent papers to sign. The patent application then went to the Washington, D.C., patent office and was promptly rejected. This patent for "improvement in fastening seams . . . in order to prevent the seam from starting or giving away from the frequent strain or pressure" was too similar to another. During the Civil War, rivets had been used to bind seams and tongues in soldiers' boots.

The examiner finally approved a revised patent in which rivets were to be used on pocket openings only. Submitted by Levi Strauss and Jacob Davis, it was granted to Davis

JACOB W. DAVIS, FORMERLY A
NEVADA TAILOR, ABOUT 1900

on May 20, 1873, and assigned to him and to Levi Strauss & Co. They were now business partners, although Jacob would soon sell a half-interest on his patent to Levi Strauss & Co.

Jacob had been continuing to sell his pants even while waiting for the patent. The pants became more and more popular as word spread about their durability. In March, even before receiving the patent, Jacob had sold all of the pants he had in stock. The following month he closed his shop in Reno and moved to San Francisco.

Now his partners had to reach a decision. Where and how were they going to manufacture the waist pantaloons, or overalls, as Levi always called them? Before this, much of the company's manufacturing had been done out of the New York headquarters, arranged for by Jonas and Louis in the tradition of the day. They hired contractors, who, in turn, hired sewing-machine operators. The operators worked at home and were paid for each completed piece of work. Levi Strauss & Co. could continue in this manner, using the willing immigrants of New York City, or find similar workers in the San Francisco area. They decided on the latter since whatever they might save employing New York's tenement dwellers would be lost in transporting the product to California.

The company put a hundred seamstresses to work in their homes in and around San Francisco. Jacob supervised the cutting of yardage and its delivery to the seamstresses' homes each morning and the pickup of the finished pantaloons each evening.

One month after the first completed pantaloons had been delivered, the partners realized they were not going to be able to keep up with the orders. They had to organize a more modern method of manufacture.

The company now opened a separate manufacturing plant, but, with Jacob Davis in charge, the actual method of operation didn't change. The only difference was the location. Sixty women now gathered in one place, a small building on Fremont Street, and each one completed entire garments. They all stitched both trousers and jackets, then made buttonholes and hammered on rivets. They were paid an average of three dollars a day. By the end of 1873, they had sold over eighteen hundred dozen pants and coats for more than forty-three thousand dollars.

If Jacob and Levi had known more about manufacturing then, they might have tried the specialization methods that were now showing more efficiency and profit in the East. There, manufacturers found that specialization brought speed. If one worker was responsible for one part of the job while another worker was responsible for another, the jobs became routine and the output became greater. Sometime later Levi would adopt this method of manufacture.

In the midst of this phenomenal success, Levi's brother-in-law David Stern died on January 2, 1874, at the home he shared with Levi and the rest of his family. Described in his obituary as "the highly respected pioneer merchant," David had been the first of the family to arrive in San Francisco and realize the possibilities there. He was buried by the Eureka Benevolent Society, the Jewish welfare and burial agency for which he had served as secretary and to which Levi contributed generously.

David's death was not the first in the family since they had come to the United States. Older sister Mary, formerly called Mathilde, had died seven years earlier, leaving her husband William Sahlein and three children. Later in 1874, Fanny Stern married William, and the combined families lived together in the house on Powell Street. There were now thirteen in all. Because the neighborhood had grown so commercial, William soon bought a new house at Post and Leavenworth, only four blocks away. When the new Sahlein family moved there, Levi moved with them.

Company sales continued to climb, with nearly two hundred thousand dollars reported in 1876. Although the company now advertised its clothing, there seemed to be little need, because demand nearly kept up with supply. Usually the company was able to keep only a week's supply on its shelves. More workers were needed, but Levi couldn't find enough white women in San Francisco to do the work. Little by little, they were turning to more genteel and higher paying positions, serving as maids in mansions of the wealthy. Since white women were still in the majority, they could just about pick and choose their jobs.

More and more manufacturers in San Francisco were turning to Chinese labor, although Levi refused to exploit Chinese workers. They were still being paid only a dollar a day and continued to work seven days a week under deplorable conditions, usually in cramped, filthy quarters in Chinatown. Levi's rivals felt it was the only way they could compete with the cheap labor so available in the East.

The one Chinese employed by Levi Strauss & Co. at this time was probably the most important person in the factory outside of Levi. All day long this man did nothing but cut, using a long knife, through many layers of tough denim and duck material. The job took strength and endurance, and the Chinese cutter stayed after many white men had tried it and quit.

Chinese labor had been a presence in California for many years. In 1848, there were only three Chinese in San Francisco. Four years later, more than twenty thousand had arrived, a few of them by sampan. Half of this number would find employment laying tracks for the Central Pacific railroad. Thousands more worked in menial jobs as laundrymen, miners, houseboys, and stevedores in and around San Francisco. Their presence was tolerated, if not welcomed, by the white laborers who would not do the work performed by the Celestials and therefore no threat was felt from the Chinese at that time.

BUILDING THE TRANSCONTINENTAL RAILROAD, A WORK TRAIN
IN 1865.

These Chinese immigrants unknowingly established in San Francisco one of the largest Chinese settlements outside of the Orient. By 1854, a semi-weekly newspaper called the *Golden Hills News* was published for them. A bilingual newspaper, *The Oriental*, followed a year later. A Chinese theater was soon established, with many retail stores and restaurants clustered nearby. The first Chinese laundry was established in 1851, and twenty years later there were two thousand. By changing crews and signs, two laundries could occupy the same space, working around the clock. By 1870, Chinese businessmen paid the greater share of monthly taxes levied on foreigners, one quarter of the state's total revenue. It's easy to understand why the state legislature printed four thousand copies of the law in Chinese.

On May 10, 1869, the last railroad spike was driven at Promontory, Utah, uniting the Central Pacific railroad coming from the west and the Union Pacific railroad coming from the east. It marked the end of California's isolation, but it also marked the end of jobs for all those Chinese laborers. Some found work elsewhere, but the majority began to drift back to San Francisco. White laborers on the railroad were out of work now, too. So were other workers congregating in San Francisco as mines and businesses failed in the diggings.

In 1873, a general depression hit the country. Banks closed their doors, strikes ignited, and jobs evaporated, although Levi Strauss & Co. was hardly affected. Soon, as many as one million men would be unemployed throughout the country. Many headed west on the newfangled intercontinental railroad, hoping to find better pickings. During the winter of 1876–77, even the weather turned sour as a drought ruined spring crops. The price of available food skyrocketed for those who could afford to pay, as Levi and his family could.

As the white unemployed grew more restless, they found a collective voice in a labor organization known as the Workingman's Party, whose philosophies attacked the Chinese as well as the rich. Made up of neighborhood anti-coolie clubs, the Workingman's Party embraced a large segment of San Francisco's population and gathered in vacant sand lots to listen to fiery speeches by their leaders. On July 23, 1877, Denis Kearney, a spokesman for the party and one of the most explosive "sand-lot orators," gathered a large crowd together to hear him speak against capitalism and its barons. But he lost control of the men

CHINESE LABORERS AT WORK IN THE SIERRAS, BUILDING THE CENTRAL PACIFIC RAILROAD.

and, with cries of "On to Chinatown," the mob raged across the city and swarmed into Dupont Street. Long blaming the Chinese for taking jobs that belonged to them, the unemployed whites now acted on their festering emotions.

They sacked, looted, and smashed their way through Chinese shops and residences, finally setting fire to everything in their path as police and firemen stood by, unable to help because they were outnumbered and their water hoses were slashed. The outrage continued for the better part of three days until San Francisco finally quieted, spent of its collective emotion.

Levi and his extended family watched Chinatown burn from their new home at 621 Leavenworth Street. Even though he was financially well off during this period of depression for others, Levi understood the feelings on both sides. At one time he had been poor and unemployed, and had felt bigotry's barbs and stings. This latest outbreak of violence only showed that it could all happen again.

8

Business as Usual

Levi decided to continue hiring as many white women as he could, knowing that he would have to pay higher wages to do so. It followed that retail prices would increase in order to pay for higher labor costs. But with the higher prices, Levi wanted to assure quality and durability of his product over the cheaper imitations now being made. How to do that? Seamstresses working in the factory rather than in their homes would assure quality control. Durability would come from using the best materials available.

The company soon was producing one hundred thousand pieces of clothing a year. Jackets and overalls with the

trademark rivets could be purchased in off-white or tan duck and indigo-dyed denim. Both colors shrank to fit, and it became very popular among the wearers, soon after purchase, to jump into the nearest stream or horse tank and immediately shrink their new pants to their own proportions.

A single New England mill furnished the denim, which meant that Levi Strauss & Co. was assured of a standard dark blue color. One mill's indigo blue could be quite different from another's. Denim originally had been woven in Nimes, France, and once was called *serge de Nimes*. Due to faulty pronunciation and a natural ellipsis, the name of the cloth soon evolved into "denim."

It also helped the quality of the product that Levi was a part owner of the oldest woolen mill on the Pacific Coast.

Late in 1875, Levi and two friends had purchased the Mission and Pacific Woolen Mills from the estate of bankrupt silver king William Ralston. The mill had long supplied Levi's company with woolen blankets and yard goods from Australia, California, and Oregon. Now the woolen mill also provided the lining for the patented riveted clothing.

Although many people assumed that these newly riveted pants were the first jeans, they were not. The first jeans were the pants that Levi had sold from his pack thirty years earlier when he tramped the hills of New York and Kentucky. They were woven of a lighter material first made in Genoa, Italy. The story has been handed down that this same material was used as sails on Columbus's ships and as pants worn by Italian sailors. Soon the word "Genoese" to describe the cloth and the pants evolved into "jeans." The use of the word to describe Levi's pants came many years later.

Jacob Davis used orange thread for the stitching to match the unique rivets on the pants and jackets. So that customers could easily tell Levi's pants from those of his competitors, the operators sewed two rows of stitches in two curving V's on the back pocket. Although this was not registered as a trademark until 1942, the company claimed that it had been used since 1873, making it the oldest clothing trademark still in use.

A guarantee, made of oilcloth, was tacked to the seat of the pants, and it promised "a new pair FREE" if the present pair ripped. A second label, made of leather, was added in 1886 and permanently stitched to the pants in the same orange thread as the V's.

Sales continued to increase, despite Levi's higher prices. Advertised as "excellently adapted to the use of those engaged in manual labor," Levi's jeans became the choice of miners, cowboys, teamsters and lumberjacks. These Double X pants, now known by the lot number 501, have remained in the line from that time to the present. Although most of the company's sales of riveted clothing occurred on the Pacific Coast, there were sales representatives in Mexico, the Hawaiian islands, and New Zealand to take care of the demand in those areas.

The year 1881 was a time of family sorrow as Louis Strauss, one of Levi's older brothers, died. Then William Sahlein died too, leaving Fanny a widow again. Jonas, the oldest of all the brothers, was nearly retired from the business. That left only Levi of the older generation.

He decided to rely more now on the Stern brothers, Fanny and David's sons, to run the ever-growing Levi Strauss & Co. Jacob, the eldest, and his younger brother, Louis, had joined the company a couple of years before.

Now Sigmund, who was thought to be the favorite nephew, also joined the company as a buyer. Abraham, the youngest, was still considered too young.

In 1886, Levi ended the old partnership and turned over the day-to-day running of business to the four Stern brothers. He spent less time there as he turned to other interests, some as interesting as the dry-goods business.

He had been a charter member and treasurer of the San Francisco Board of Trade since 1877, serving on a special committee lobbying Congress for a Central American canal. A canal would not only shorten the time to the Eastern market for California products, but make them more profitable as well. The committee unanimously endorsed a Nicaraguan route, which it preferred to a Panamanian course of travel. Nothing happened in that area for thirty-four years, however, until George Washington Geothals engineered the canal in Panama.

EARLY CATTLE ROUNDUP SHOWS CATTLEMEN IN DOUBLE X WAIST OVERALLS.

Transportation and communication had been on Levi's mind since the early days of his business when he had to wait months for a letter or a shipment of goods from back East.

In the early days of the gold rush, a shipment of mail arriving in San Francisco created a scene of extraordinary excitement. Lines of two hundred people or more formed

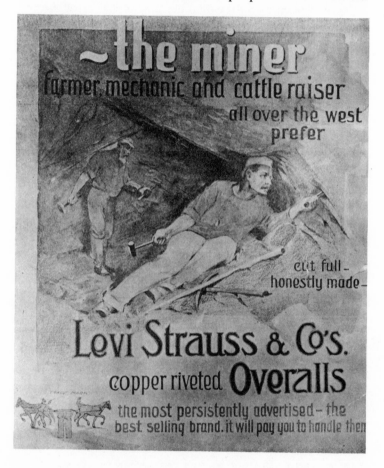

EARLY 1900s ADVERTISEMENTS FOR LEVI STRAUSS JEANS.

by daybreak. Barricades were often needed to keep the more eager recipients outside until the doors of the post office opened.

Some of the city's more enterprising citizens soon realized that money could be made even from this. Paying twenty-five cents a letter to the San Francisco postmaster, a man named Alexander Todd bought the privilege of enter-

ing the building directly and sorting out the mail for his subscribers. Other people paid as much as twenty dollars for someone to stand in line for them. Still others queued up early, then sold their places for outrageous sums.

Soon the mail delivery business combined with the gold safekeeping business. Wells Fargo, organized to deliver mail in 1852, became a banking business as well. Twice a month the Pacific Mail Line left with shipments of gold from the East, and it became the custom for businessmen to settle accounts on Steamer Day.

As Levi's business slowly expanded in the late 1850s, cross-country stagecoach freight service grew to match. Occasionally Levi was able to take advantage of the overland train's eight deliveries a month, although most of the freight continued to be moved from one coast to another by sea.

Other attempts to move mail and cargo were unusual at best in those early days. The Army-run camel express turned out to be a comedy of errors involving frustrated Arabian camels who understood no English and drivers who spoke no camel. Dog teams showed they could pull heavy loads over snow-laden passes, but the loads were limited in size. A man named "Snowshoe" Thompson tried out for the job, too, and skied through the Sierra with a one-hundred-pound sack of mail strapped to his back, proving it could be done. For two winters, Thompson was the lifeline to civilization for many snowbound settlers until a regular service was established.

In April 1860, two enterprising men and a team of vigorous horses began the Pony Express. It lasted for eighteen months and was by far the most famous of all the schemes, although the amount of mail actually handled was small and, again, limited in size. It was also expensive, costing five dollars per half ounce, When the telegraph came to San Francisco in 1861, the Pony Express galloped into history.

The transcontinental railroad became a fact in 1869, but it favored east-to-west transportation by charging unusually high freight rates from west-to-east. San Francisco's merchants felt limited in their Eastern dealings and concentrated sales on the Pacific Coast until that, too, was threatened. The railroad tycoons who were responsible for the Central Pacific railroad going east had now built the Southern Pacific going south. Soon, San Francisco's position of a central trading headquarters was threatened by freight rates that made it more attractive to ship goods through Los Angeles to California's central valley.

In 1891, Levi Strauss decided to go into the railroad business. Despite opposition from the railroad and a corrupt legislature, a group of forty San Francisco businessmen put up one thousand dollars each to survey a possible railroad line. Levi was one of the forty. When this venture failed, they tried again two years later. This time each man subscribed twenty-five thousand dollars to build a railroad through California's central valley.

This railroad was more successful, but after the line was completed to the southern tip of the San Joaquin Valley, it was sold to the Atchison, Topeka and Santa Fe railroad without the consent of stockholders like Levi. It then formed an agreement with the Southern Pacific railroad to form a profitable monopoly. Soon after that, Levi retired from his unsuccessful venture into the railroad business.

But he never lacked for things to do. He was a director of many companies and corporations. The Nevada Bank, the Union Trust Company, and the San Francisco Gas Company were but a few of the business organizations that sought his advice and leadership on their boards. Then there was the matter of real estate.

One publication of his day noted:

From time to time he (Levi) invested his surplus funds in city property and became one of the potent factors in building the city. Many of the substantial business blocks on Kearny, Market, Post, Powell, Sansome, and other streets (the very core of commercial San Francisco) were built by him. He has bought, built, and sold much property, and is still the owner of valuable holdings.

If Levi Strauss had thoughts of retiring at this time, his actions never displayed it. He had left Bavaria many years ago as a penniless teenager, a *Yehud* without a trade. He had come to America, the promised land, where opportunity knocked for everyone. As far as he was concerned, the knocking on his own front door hadn't stopped yet.

9

"A Willing and Hopeful Heart"

SAN FRANCISCO CALL

Levi Straus was sixty-six in 1895, old for a man living in the nineteenth century. He had outlived even some of the second generation of his family who had come to California, the land of the golden mountains.

His philosophy about his life, his goals and even his loneliness came out in a rare interview he gave the San Francisco *Bulletin* in October. It is probably Strauss's only known interview, since he was a private man who shunned publicity.

"I am a bachelor," he said, "and I fancy on that account I need to work more, for my entire life is my business. I don't believe that a man who once forms the habit of being busy can retire and be contented . . . My happiness lies in my routine work."

Then he went on to say, "I do not think large fortunes cause happiness to their owners, for immediately those who possess them become slaves to their wealth. They must devote their lives to caring for their possessions. I don't

LEVI STRAUSS, DATE UNKNOWN.

think money brings friends to its owner. In fact, often the result is quite the contrary."

His attention now turned to his philanthropies. Jacob Stern, his nephew, was a trustee of the Pacific Hebrew Orphan Asylum and Home, and Levi became a major contributor to it. He also continued to donate to the Eureka Benevolent Society, an organization that had been a favorite of David Stern's. The society also maintained a permanent tie with the Hebrew Board of Relief.

In 1897, Levi Strauss began his association with the University of California. Jacob Reinstein, a close friend and a regent of the university, asked Levi to contribute toward the school's scholarship fund. Levi replied with a proposal of his own. He offered to match the legislature's creation of twenty-eight perpetual scholarships, four from each congressional district in the state. Privately, Levi also helped many young people in whom he had taken an interest with financial gifts to continue their higher education.

Writing in *San Francisco Society* in 1887, Mary Watson concluded that no community in the city was so wide and unbounded in its charities as the Jewish community. No matter what the cause, Jewish or otherwise, the Jews in San Francisco were seldom appealed to in vain. There were many Christian charitable societies whose managers freely admitted the extent of Jewish contributions that had helped them over financial hurdles. In fact, it was widely felt that contributions by its Jewish citizens to all aspects of life—charitable, cultural, educational, and economic—had brought a stabilizing effect to San Francisco at a time when the rest of the state was anything but stable. Genuine acceptance by their fellow citizens must have seemed unusual at first to a group of people whose inheritance included persecution, but they warmed to this acceptance and responded by dropping their traditional exclusivity.

As stated by B. E. Lloyd in *Lights and Shade in San Francisco*, published in 1876:

> In California, Catholic and Protestant, Jew and Gentile, all seem to have united in the one effort of establishing a civilization on a broad and liberal foundation, the rules of which would not restrict in any way the liberties of any, so long as they observed the acknowledged principles of right.

Although the *Elite Directory of 1879* segregated their names under the title "Jewish Address List," by 1888 the city's first *Blue Book* listed all the city's socially elite alphabetically, without distinction.

Levi was seventy-three in 1902 and had not felt well during the past year. He seemed to have heart trouble, though the diagnosis was vague. Seeking a change, he went to the Hotel Del Monte in Monterey to spend a week resting with other wealthy, but ailing, Americans.

When he returned to the city, he stayed busy with many business details. He went to the factory, too, just to look and perhaps marvel at the business he had founded. One lady, a former seamstress at the Fremont Street factory, remembered his visits.

"He used to come to the door of the big room where we all worked and look it over. He never came in; he just gave the room a once-over. He always wore dark suits and carried a tall hat in his hand," she said.

On Friday, September 19, 1902, he completed a new will. Levi would give twenty thousand dollars to the Pacific Hebrew Orphan Asylum, ten thousand dollars to the Home for Aged Israelites, five thousand dollars to the Eureka Benevolent Association, and five thousand dollars each to the Roman Catholic and Protestant orphanages. In all, he would give away $1.6 million to charities, friends, children, and grandchildren of his brothers and sisters, payable in gold. To Fanny's four sons, Jacob, Sigmund, Louis, and

Abraham, he left his company and the rest of the $6 million estate.

He worked in his Battery Street office on Monday after he signed his new will. The following day he went home early, complaining that he didn't feel well. His nephews' wives called the doctor, who sent him to bed with some-

CATALOG PAGE ADVERTISING NEW LINE OF LEVI'S PANTS.

thing he diagnosed as congestion of the liver. On Friday evening Levi felt well enough to get up and eat dinner with his family and enjoy their company. That night he awoke with some discomfort.

His nurse asked him how he felt, and he replied, "About as comfortable as I can under the circumstances." A few minutes later he was dead.

The city mourned his death with his family and friends. Flags flew at half-mast, and his obituary appeared in all the city newspapers. The San Francisco *Call* printed a story about his life and career that ran three columns. It stated:

> With small capital, but with a clear head, a willing and hopeful heart, he opened up the house of Levi Strauss & Co. dry goods and merchandise, as the head and principal owner of which he remained until his death nearly forty-nine years later.

At a special meeting of the Board of Trade directors the following afternoon, members called for resolutions honoring Levi. One of the resolutions stated that

> By the death of Mr. Strauss, the state of California loses one of its foremost and high-minded citizens; the city of San Francisco, a pioneer merchant whose success was only equaled by his good deeds and unblemished reputation; and this association, a member whose labors, patience, fortitude, and good judgment are imperishably inscribed in its records.
>
> That the great causes of education and charity have likewise suffered a signal loss in the death of Mr. Strauss, whose splendid endowments to the University of California will be an enduring testimonial of his worth as a liberal, public-minded citizen and whose numberless unostentatious acts of charity in which neither race nor creed were recognized, exemplified his broad and generous love for and sympathy with humanity.

The funeral at ten-thirty on Monday was conducted by Rabbi Jacob Voorsanger of Temple Emanu-El. Businesses were closed by official declaration so that Levi's friends and associates could attend the simple, yet moving, ceremony at his home on Leavenworth Street.

After the services, two hundred employees from Levi Strauss & Co. acted as escort for Levi's casket, which was carried in stately procession through San Francisco streets to the Southern Pacific railroad station. A special funeral train waited there to transport him to the Home of Peace cemetery in Colma.

Eulogies continued to be written and printed long after his death, reminding readers that they should not forget Levi, who had contributed much to the city and country of which he was an honored member.

And he never has been forgotten through the years. Today, around the world, nearly everyone knows his name. He is remembered, however, not for his intelligence and hard-work ethic, nor for his generosity and spirit of good will. Rather, it is because of a simple, yet durable, pair of pants that his name lives on. Levi's. Perhaps it is enough.

10

Epilogue
An Ending and a Beginning

The nation and businesses like Levi Strauss & Co. were changing and growing together as the twentieth century moved into its sixth year. A young president named Theodore Roosevelt occupied the White House. He had energy to match his enthusiasm and was leading the nation with a vigor such as Levi once displayed in running his company. The climate in the country grew healthy for business.

Although Levi the man was gone now, his nephews, the Stern brothers, were determined to keep the company moving along the same avenue of progress their uncle had traveled. The eldest brother, Jacob, was an efficient and benevolent president. Sales of jeans had increased from year to year since Levi's death, despite the work of imitators capitalizing on the jeans look. The Sterns felt comfortable and perhaps a bit complacent with the outlook of the business they had inherited from Uncle Levi.

And then something happened to shake them, literally as well as figuratively, from their complacency. Early risers in San Francisco on the morning of April 18, 1906, might have questioned the nervous stamping of horses, the howling and barking of dogs. Even if they had, however, no one could have predicted the magnitude of what followed.

With one explosive motion, an earthquake slashed through the coastline north and south of the city. It demolished small settlements, ripped open the ocean floor, uprooted ancient redwoods, crumbled the stone quadrangle of Stanford University, and snapped the pipes of the Peninsula Reservoir that held the reserve water supply for San Francisco. Then, traveling at seven thousand miles an hour, the quake hit San Francisco with devastating fury at 5:12 A.M.

"There was a deep rumble," said Jesse Cook, a police sergeant who was on duty that morning, ". . . and then I could actually see it coming up Washington Street. The whole street was undulating . . ."

A long, low moaning sound prevailed as the city was wrenched from its foundations. Buildings shook, glass shattered, wood ripped, masonry cracked. Church bells began to ring as if sounding the city's death knell. Finally, after approximately forty long seconds, the quaking diminished for ten seconds, then it began again for another twenty-five seconds. It stopped, and there was only an ominous silence everywhere, except for the steady hiss of gas escaping from broken lines.

Sigmund Stern and his wife, Rosalie, were asleep in their large home near Van Ness Avenue when the tremor woke them. They dressed quickly and checked the house. It

seemed to be damaged only slightly. Rosalie instructed the servants to begin cleaning up the books fallen from shelves in the library and the broken crockery fallen from shelves in the kitchen.

After breakfast, Sigmund hurried to the Levi Strauss & Co. office at 14–16 Battery Street to assess its possible damage. Only five feet, four inches tall, Sigmund was a particular dresser and known around the factory as "The Little Prince." Today, he could not have been blamed if his attire was less than perfect.

The streets were gashed with twisted trolley tracks and

A VIEW DOWN SACRA-
MENTO STREET FROM
POWELL, AFTER THE SAN
FRANCISCO EARTHQUAKE.

fallen cornices. Great chunks of pavement were lifted along the fault line, preventing any newfangled automobiles, like the Stern's Pope-Toledo limousine, from being used. Sigmund Stern picked his way to Battery Street, probably by horse and carriage.

Fires already burned south of Market Street by the time Sigmund approached the business district. Many buildings burned out of control, sending bright flames into the clear morning sky. The Battery Street building was no exception. It had been ignited by the shattered gaslight chandelier Levi had proudly installed so many years before.

Broken water mains contributed to the helplessness and frustration everyone felt as the work of many lifetimes went up in smoke.

In Chinatown, more drama unfolded as a huge bull, bawling with pain and fear, lurched through the streets. For many of the Celestials, the animal was living proof of their belief that the world was supported on the backs of four bulls. This one had left his post, causing the earth to tremble. Now the crowds began to hit him with stones, knives, anything at all, to drive him back to his position. Wounded and near death, the huge animal stumbled past tenements and stores into Portsmouth Square, where a police officer killed him.

The fire in the city gathered momentum now as Rosalie Stern took charge of family matters. First, she ordered her sister, Elise, wife of another Stern brother, Abraham, to go to Jacob's home. He and his family were vacationing in Europe and had a house full of valuable paintings to be rescued. Elise and Abraham brought the priceless art to Sigmund and Rosalie's house.

That done, the combined Stern families gathered at Sigmund's to camp in the yard outside. The roof of his house threatened to collapse with each aftershock.

During the night, the fires in the city burned closer. The next morning the family joined other bedraggled refugees gathered for safety in the parade ground at the Presidio. The next day they moved again, to Golden Gate Park. Here they all huddled together—leaders of business and society, children, maids, nannies, and butlers—to cook over campfires and listen to the thud of dynamite as city officials leveled a firebreak at Van Ness Avenue.

On the third day, firefighters, with the help of shifting winds and, finally, rain, contained the inferno. At exactly 7:15 A.M., seventy-four hours after it had begun, the great fire of San Francisco burned itself out. Damage to property was estimated at $500 million, and 478 people were known dead. The fate of countless others remained unknown as one third of the city smoldered in ruins.

Before the ashes cooled, Abraham and Sigmund Stern were hard at work. Using Abraham's home for an office, since it had been damaged only slightly, they began to pull the tattered remains of the business together. Quickly they repaired their Oakland factory to be used as headquarters for the goods that brother Louis would ship from the East.

MEDIUM WEIGHT   LIGHT WEIGHT FAST COLOR   HICKORY STRIPE HEAVY   LIGHT WEIGHT FAST COLOR

LIGHT WEIGHT FAST COLOR   LIGHT WEIGHT FAST COLOR   BLUE DENIM HEAVY   LIGHT WEIGHT FAST COLOR

ALL KOVERALLS ARE MADE IN EITHER DUTCH NECK AND ELBOW SLEEVES OR HIGH NECK AND LONG SLEEVES.   SIZES - 1 TO 8 YEARS.

PAGE FROM A COMPANY CATALOG ADVERTISING KOVERALLS

By the time Jacob Stern returned home from Europe, Abraham and Sigmund were supervising the building of a new factory on Valencia Street. In the planning stage was another building to replace the Battery Street headquarters lost in the fire.

Now they also made two decisions that were characteristic of the way Levi had always done business. First, they extended credit to all retail merchants wiped out in the earthquake. Second, they notified their 350 employees that they would remain on salary. Some employees were put to work immediately, but others did not return to work until September. Their salaries, however, remained constant.

Throughout the years that followed, the business grew as new products were successfully added. Play clothes for children, called Koveralls, were introduced. It was the first time sturdy play clothes had been manufactured for youngsters, and they became instantly popular. Old Jacob Davis's three-year-old granddaughter became the Koverall girl in the advertising.

Production also changed at this time as the company installed its first automated assembly line. Jacob Stern went to Detroit to see what Henry Ford was doing at his automobile plant and came back to adapt Ford's system to the sewing of clothes.

The Depression of the thirties hit Levi Strauss & Co. as it did most American industries. People couldn't afford to buy new clothes, so warehouses filled with jeans and other denim merchandise. The assembly lines slowed down or quit altogether, but the company kept its employees working by having them repair, refurbish, and modernize the Valencia Street plant.

Until now, blue jeans were primarily western clothing, worn by cowboys and other outdoorsmen who needed their durability and strength. With the Depression, however, many hard-hit western ranches found a way to attract new

A MACHINE OPERATOR IN THE KOVERALL FAC-
TORY AROUND 1919.

income. They opened their doors to "dudes," folks from back East who could afford a different vacation.

Vacationers bought jeans for ranch use and took them home for leisure wear. Then Levi's jeans began to show up in Eastern stores, and the company took out its first national ad.

World War II brought a temporary halt to the popularity of jeans. Material shortages made their manufacture "an essential industry," and only those engaged in defense work were allowed to buy the limited quantity turned out by the company.

After World War II ended, the demand for Levi's grew faster than the supply. When stores put up signs saying "Levi's Today," customers lined up to wait for the doors to open. Recognizing this demand as the edict of the future, the company prepared for national and international sales and distribution. In the years since, more than two billion pairs of Levi's have been sold worldwide.

Today, jeans are an American tradition, originating more than one hundred years ago in the dreams of an immigrant from Bavaria. Levi Strauss's achievement has often been called the classical American success story, and no one can disagree, for it is just that. A classic.

Bibliography

Chidsey, Donald Barr. *California Gold Rush.* New York: Crown Publishers, 1968.

Cray, Ed. *Levi's.* Boston: Houghton Mifflin Company, 1978.

Golden, Harry. *Forgotten Pioneer.* New York: World Publishing Company, 1963.

Groh, George W. *Gold Fever.* New York: William Morrow and Company, 1966.

Learsi, Rufus. *The Jews in America: A History.* New York: World Publishing Company, 1954.

Lee, W. Storrs. *The Sierra.* New York: G. P. Putnam's Sons, 1962.

Lewis, Oscar. *San Francisco: Mission to Metropolis.* Berkeley: Howell-North Books, 1966.

Muscatine, Doris. *Old San Francisco.* New York. G. P. Putnam's Sons, 1975.

Nadeau, Remi. *Ghost Towns and Mining Camps of California*. Los Angeles: Ward Ritchie Press, 1965.

Narrell, Irena. *Our City: The Jews of San Francisco*. San Diego: Howell North Publishers, 1981.

Sharfman, Dr. I. Harold. *"Nothing Left to Commemorate."* Glendale: Arthur H. Clark Company, 1969.

Thomas, Gordon and Max Morgan Witts. *The San Francisco Earthquake*. New York: Stein and Day, 1971.

Wright, Richardson. *Hawkers and Walkers*. Philadelphia: J. B. Lippincott, 1927.

INDEX